JOURNAL

PETER PAUPER PRESS, INC.
White Plains, New York

PETER PAUPER PRESS
Fine Books and Gifts Since 1928

Our Company

In 1928, at the age of twenty-two, Peter Beilenson began printing books on a small press in the basement of his parents' home in Larchmont, New York. Peter—and later, his wife, Edna—sought to create fine books that sold at "prices even a pauper could afford."

Today, still family owned and operated, Peter Pauper Press continues to honor our founders' legacy—and our customers' expectations—of beauty, quality, and value.

202 Mamaroneck Avenue
White Plains, NY 10601 USA

ISBN 978-1-4413-2942-4
Printed in China
7 6 5 4 3 2 1

Visit us at www.peterpauper.com